TIFFANY-STYLE
STAINED GLASS LAMPSHADES

With Full-Size Templates for 11 Designs

Connie Clough Eaton

DOVER PUBLICATIONS, INC.
New York

INTRODUCTION

This book contains ready-to-use full-size templates for making 11 lampshades. Stained glass lampshades of this type were first made by Louis C. Tiffany at the turn of the century, and have since become valuable and cherished heirlooms. These projects are intended for the craftsperson already familiar with the basics of the craft, so instructions on such skills as selecting and cutting glass are not provided here. Those not familiar with these skills are referred to one of the many introductions to stained glass currently available (among the best is *Stained Glass Craft* by J. A. F. Divine and G. Blachford, Dover Publications, 0-486-22812-6).

Each assembled lampshade may have 4, 6, or 8 sides, depending on the particular design. Some plates consist of several templates, and on each of these pages is provided a small illustration to show how the parts fit together to make a repeating unit. Some lampshades have skirt pieces that fit on the bottom; these require a slightly more complicated assembly. Some patterns (such as the one on Plate 28), for space reasons, have their top sections separated—don't forget to add them back in when working on the lampshades. See the inside covers of this book for color renditions of how the parts and sides fit together for each of the lamps.

HOW TO USE THE TEMPLATES

It is important to keep the edges of the heavyweight paper as neat and firm as possible, so use very sharp scissors or an X-ACTO knife when cutting out a template (you may want to remove the entire page from the book). *Trace the template onto a sheet of tracing paper before cutting the template into individual pieces.* The tracing is then used as a reference when the time comes to assemble the pieces to form a lampshade panel. Number the pieces on the template and on the tracing.

COPPER FOIL TECHNIQUE

Begin by assembling the individual panels using the copper foil technique. Use adhesive-backed copper foil, which is available in 36-yard rolls, in widths of 3/16", 1/4", 3/8" and 1/2". After cutting the glass, wrap a thin strip of foil around the edges of each piece. Make certain that the glass is centered over the foil so that it extends an equal distance on both sides of the glass. The foil strip should be long enough to go around all edges of the piece and overlap itself by about 1/4". Press the foil carefully and firmly into place using a fid, burnisher or pencil. Trim excess foil at the corners with a scissors, razor blade or X-ACTO knife.

Fit the glass pieces of an individual panel together, treating any pieces that are to hang off the bottom as separate units. Tack the corners of each piece of glass by holding a soldering iron or gun over the corners and dropping a piece of solder onto the corner. Coat the foil with a thin layer of flux and then move the soldering gun along the foil while pulling the solder close behind. On contact with the foil, the solder should melt and spread out along the entire width of the foil. Repeat this procedure with the other panels.

ASSEMBLING THE LAMPSHADE

Place all completed panels *face down* and edge-to-edge, as in Figure 1. Tack the panels together at the points indicated by the circles, using small drops of solder. Tack the hanging panel(s) to the bottom of the main panel using a bead of solder at each corner. *Do not* tack the sides of the hanging panels to each other at this time, but leave them splayed out from the main panels. Very carefully, turn the lampshade *face up*.

Grasp the two unattached sides of the assembly and bring them up so that the two edges meet and the lampshade assumes the familiar circular shape. Tack the free ends together on the outside with two drops of solder. The hanging pieces can now be pushed into place, so that their adjacent edges meet and form tiers at a different angle than the main part of the shade. Tack adjacent hanging sections at the corners.

In the same way that you soldered individual pieces together to form panels, solder all panels and hanging sections together, first on the outside, then on the inside of the lampshade. The lampshade should rest on its topside as you solder the inside, and on its bottom as you solder the outside.

Visit your local hardware or electrical supply store to see the electrical fixtures that are available and for information on how to install them. Because the shades are quite heavy, they are more suitable for hanging lamps than for table lamps.

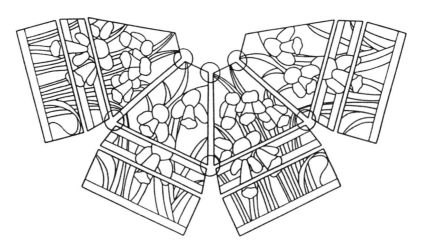

Figure 1

Tiffany-Style Stained Glass Lampshades: With Full-Size Templates for 11 Designs is a new work, first published by Dover Publications, Inc., in 1993.

Manufactured in the United States of America
Dover Publications, Inc., 31 East 2nd Street, Mineola, N.Y. 11501

Library of Congress Cataloging-in-Publication Data

Eaton, Connie.
    Tiffany-style stained glass lampshades : with full-size templates for 11 designs / Connie Clough Eaton.
        p.   cm.
        ISBN 0-486-27589-2 (pbk.)
        1. Glass craft—Patterns.   2. Glass painting and staining—Patterns.
3. Lampshades, Glass. I. Title.
TT298.E186   1993
749'.63—dc20
                        93-12325
                        CIP

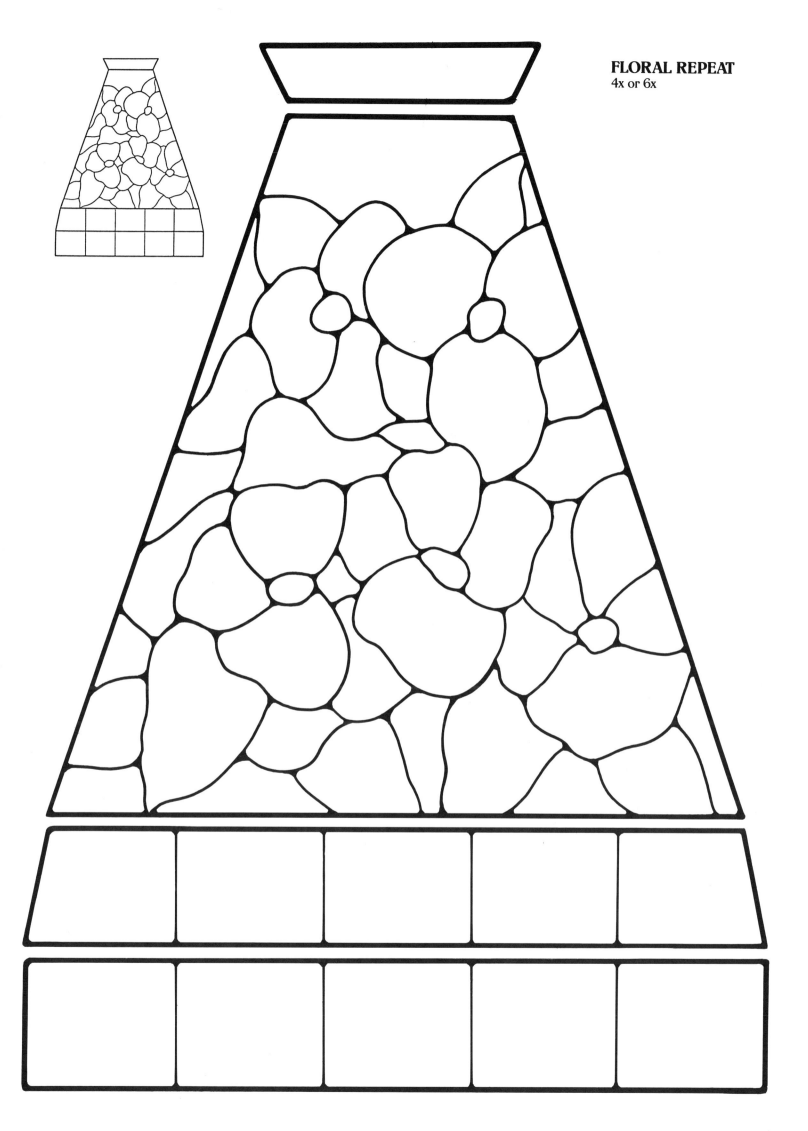

FLORAL REPEAT
4x or 6x

PLATE 1

DAFFODIL (1 of 2)
Repeat 2x each (total of 4 panels).

PLATE 2

PLATE 3

TULIP (1 of 3)
Repeat 2x each (total of 6 panels).

PLATE 4

PLATE 5

PLATE 6

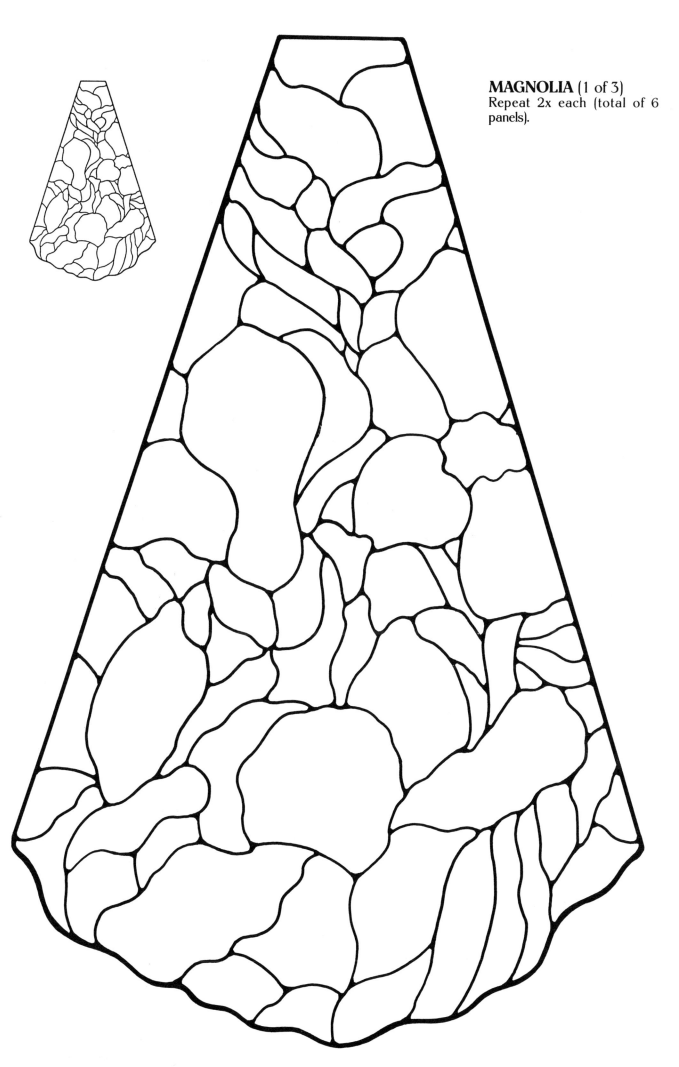

MAGNOLIA (1 of 3)
Repeat 2x each (total of 6 panels).

PLATE 7

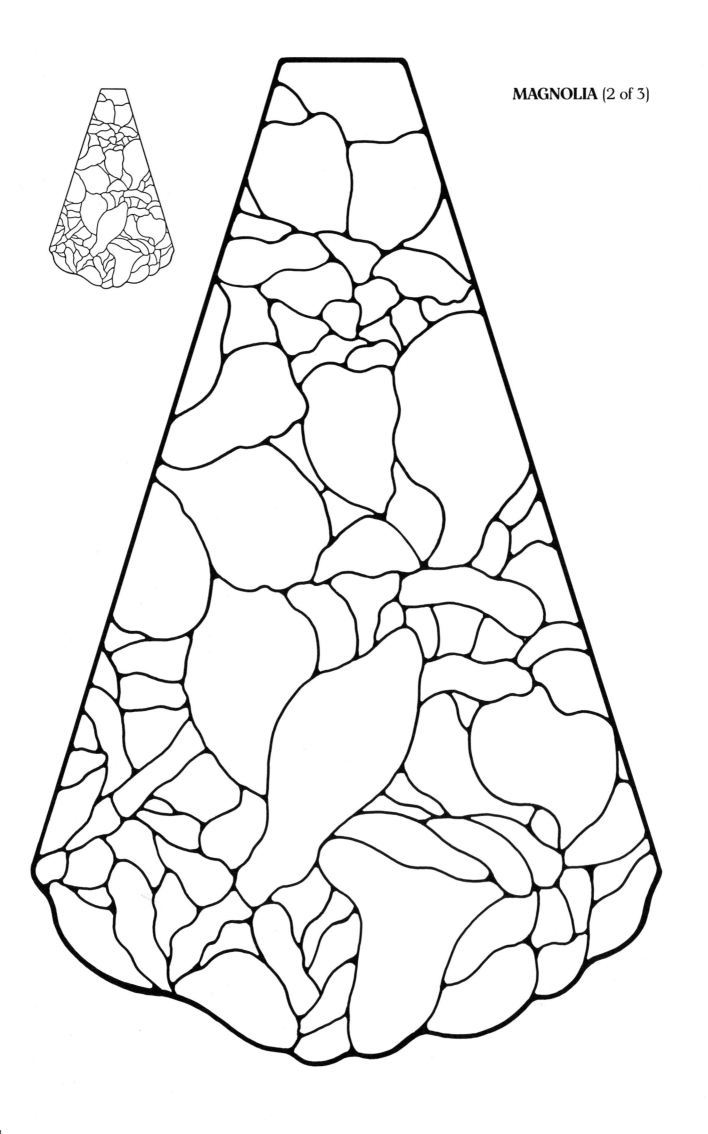

PLATE 8

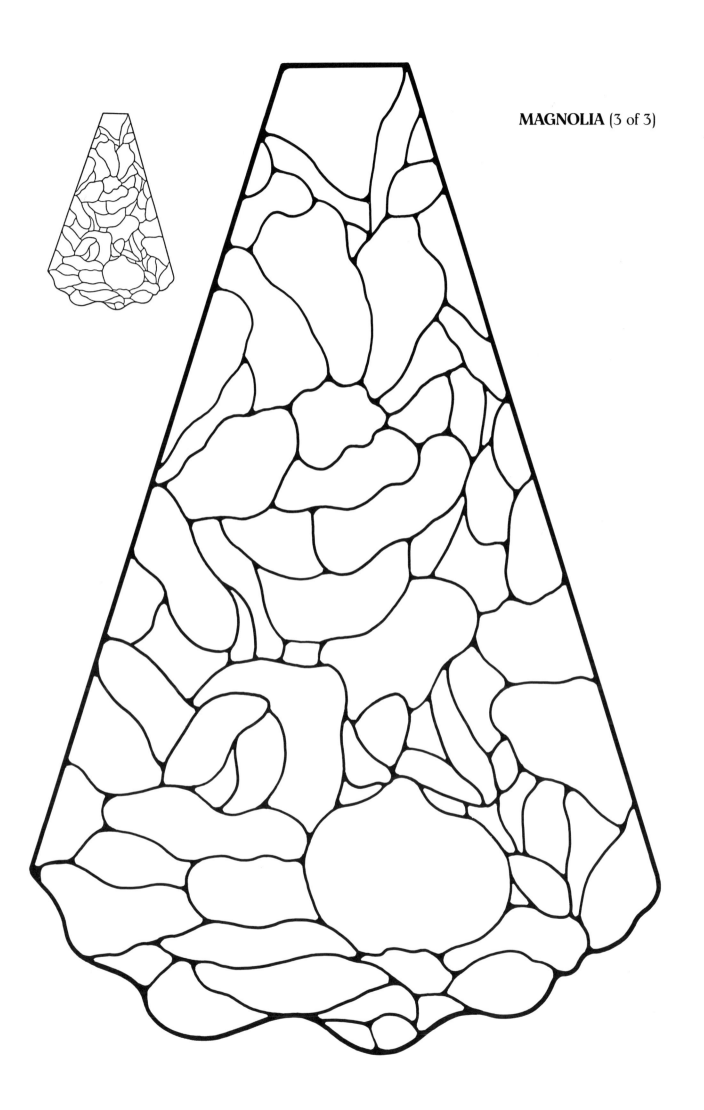

PLATE 9

POPPY (1 of 2)
Repeat 2x each (total of 4 panels).

PLATE 10

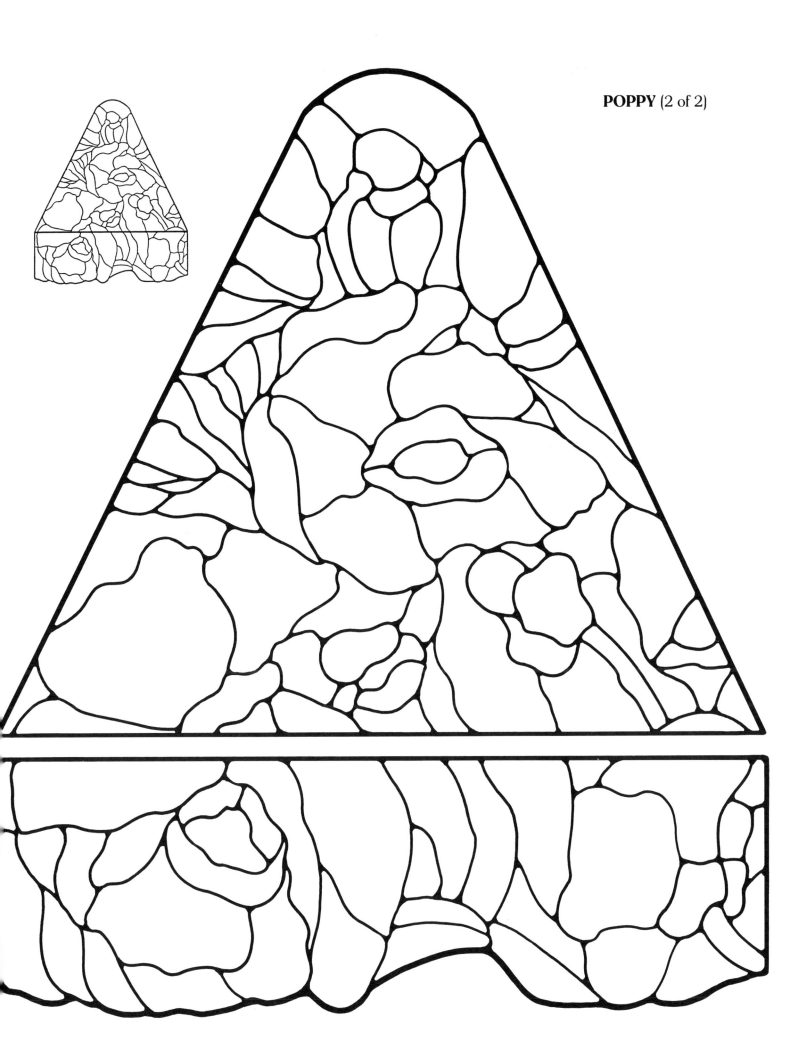

PLATE 11

DRAGONFLY (1 of 2)
Repeat 2x or 3x each (total of 4 or 6 panels).

PLATE 12

PLATE 13

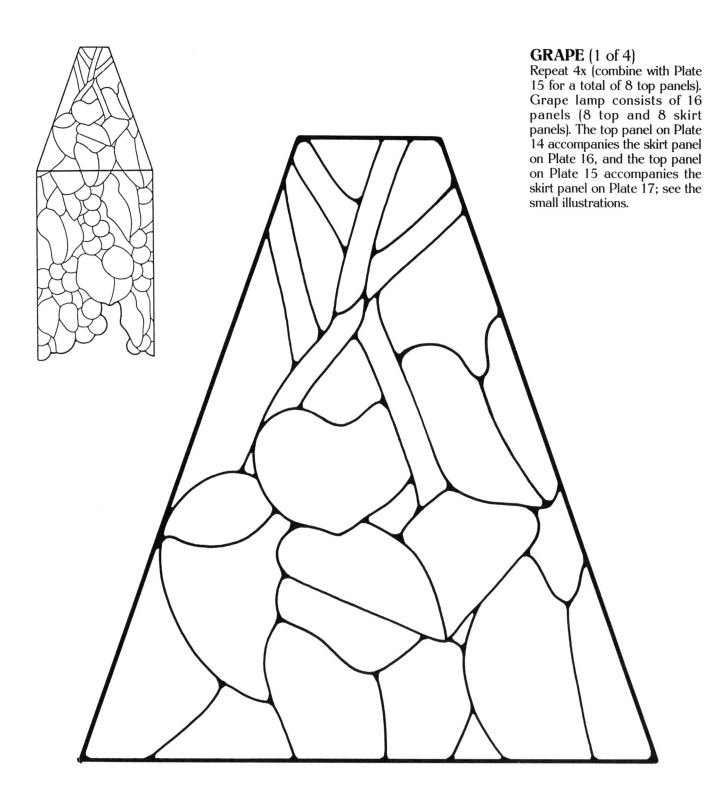

GRAPE (1 of 4)
Repeat 4x (combine with Plate 15 for a total of 8 top panels). Grape lamp consists of 16 panels (8 top and 8 skirt panels). The top panel on Plate 14 accompanies the skirt panel on Plate 16, and the top panel on Plate 15 accompanies the skirt panel on Plate 17; see the small illustrations.

PLATE 14

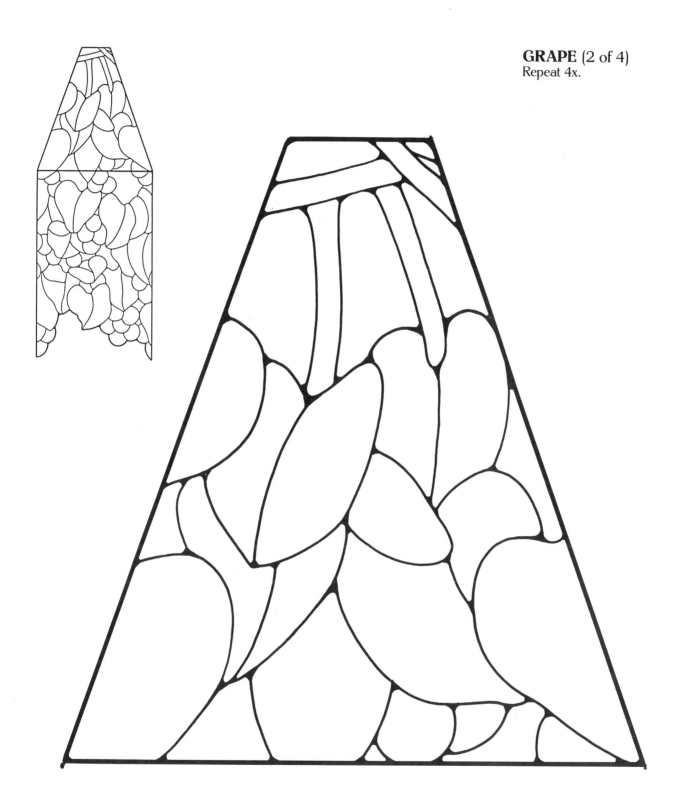

PLATE 15

GRAPE (3 of 4)
Repeat 4x (combine with Plate
17 for a total of 8 skirt panels).

PLATE 16

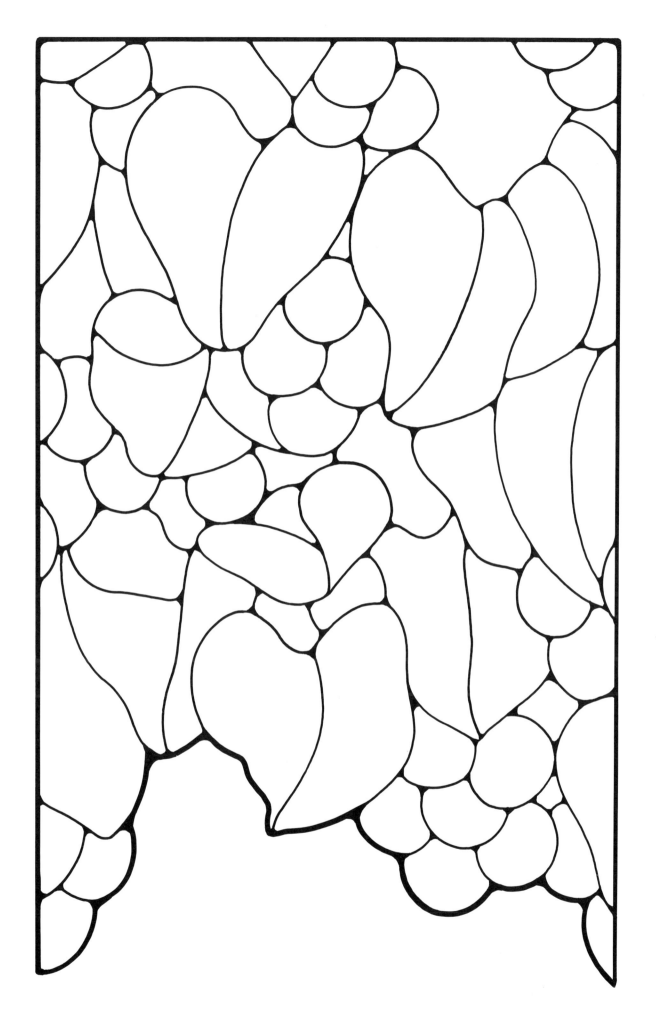

GRAPE (4 of 4)
Repeat 4x.

PLATE 17

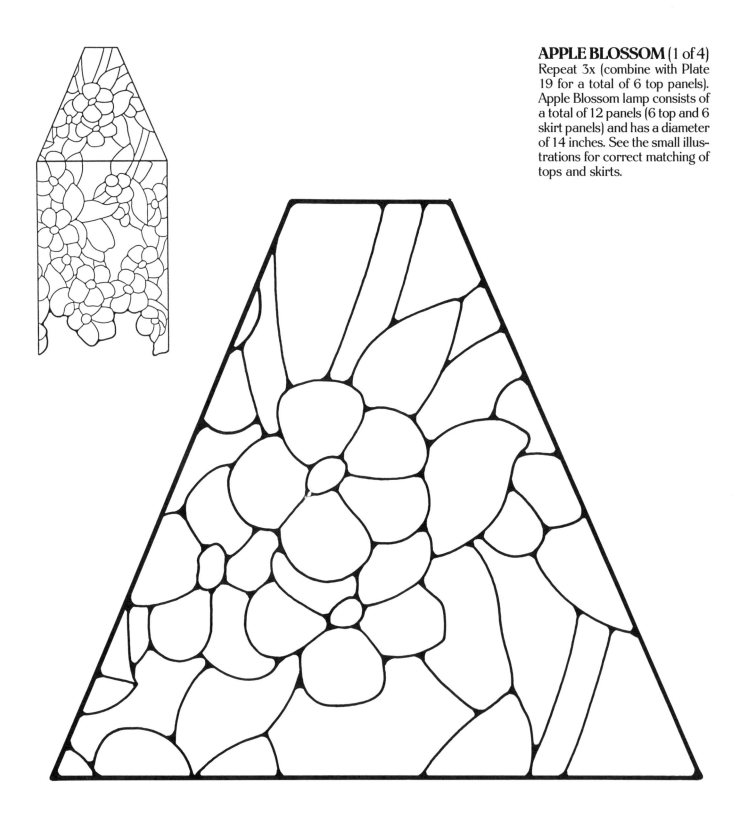

APPLE BLOSSOM (1 of 4)
Repeat 3x (combine with Plate 19 for a total of 6 top panels). Apple Blossom lamp consists of a total of 12 panels (6 top and 6 skirt panels) and has a diameter of 14 inches. See the small illustrations for correct matching of tops and skirts.

PLATE 18

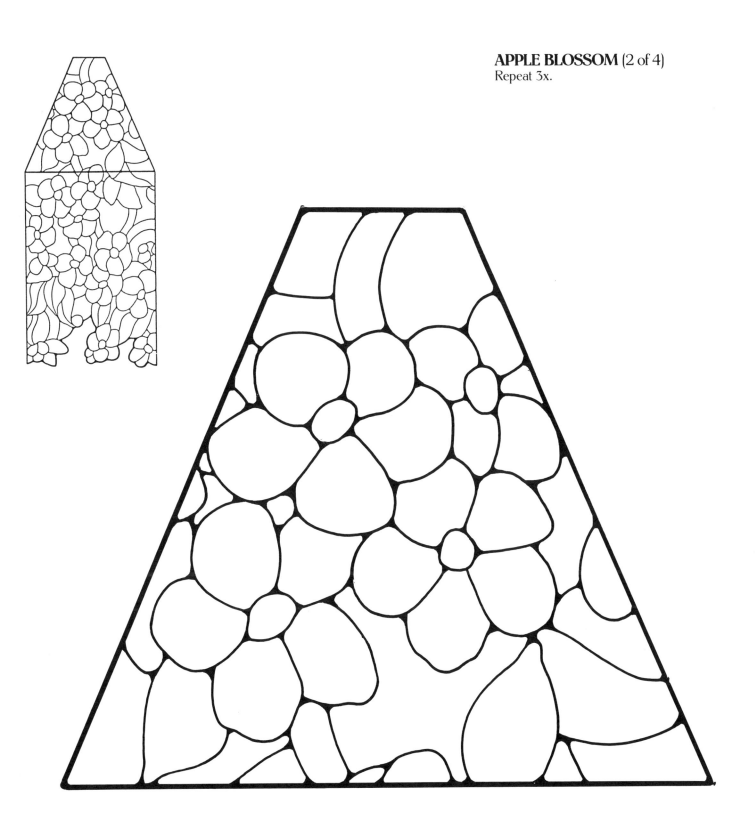

PLATE 19

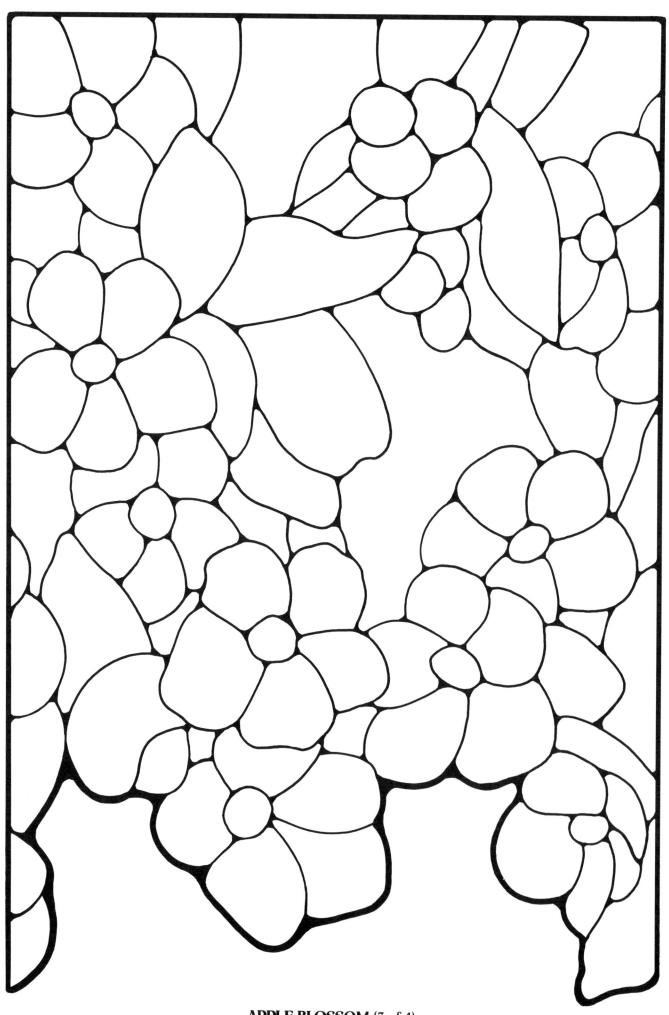

APPLE BLOSSOM (3 of 4)
Repeat 3x (combine with Plate
21 for a total of 6 skirt panels).

PLATE 20

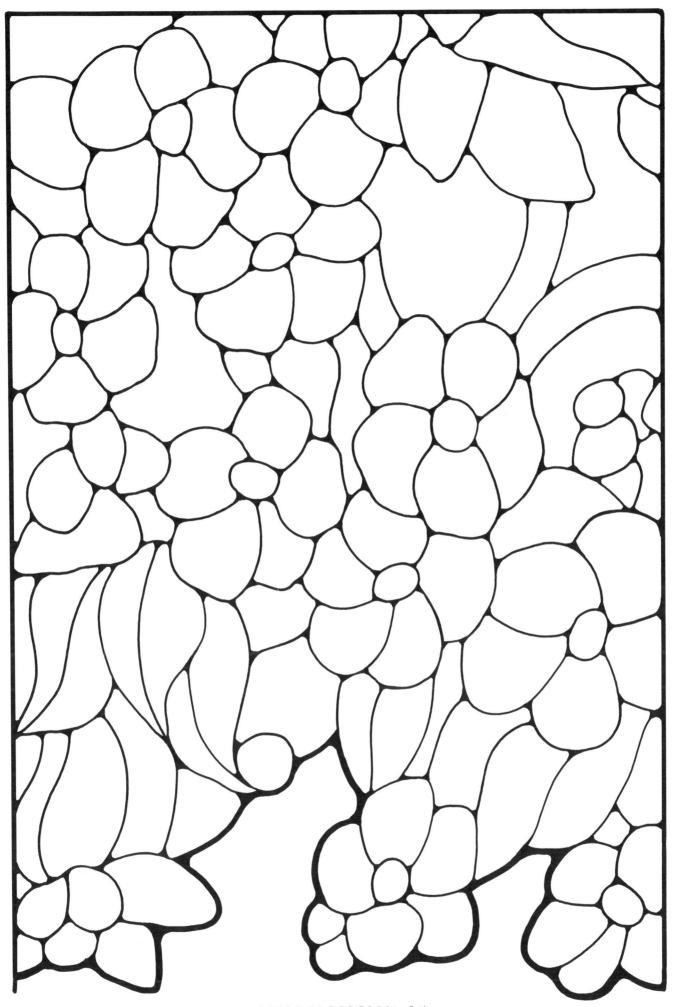

APPLE BLOSSOM (4 of 4)
Repeat 3x.

PLATE 21

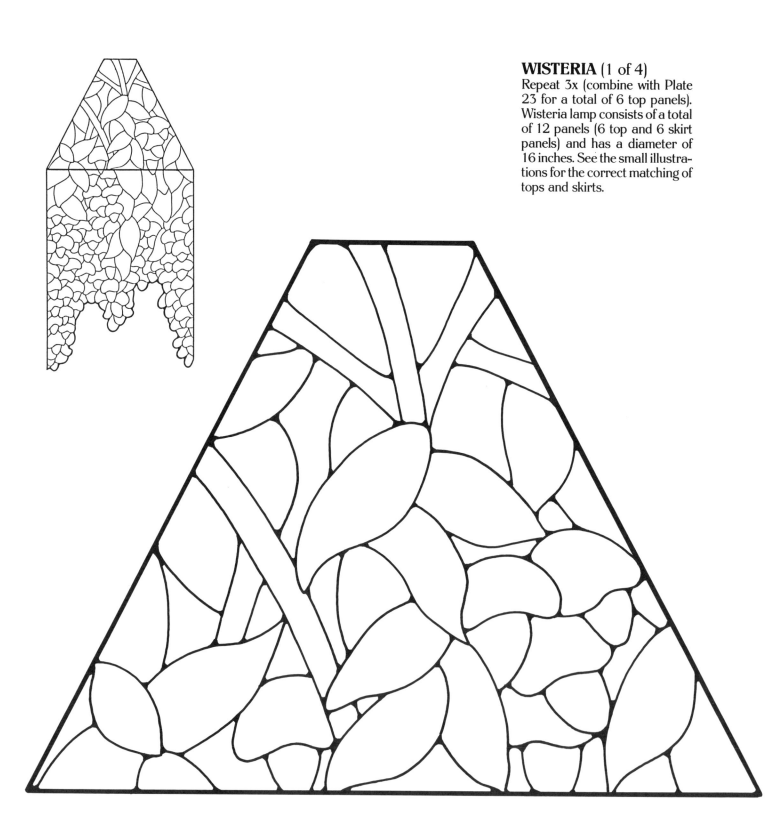

WISTERIA (1 of 4)
Repeat 3x (combine with Plate 23 for a total of 6 top panels). Wisteria lamp consists of a total of 12 panels (6 top and 6 skirt panels) and has a diameter of 16 inches. See the small illustrations for the correct matching of tops and skirts.

PLATE 22

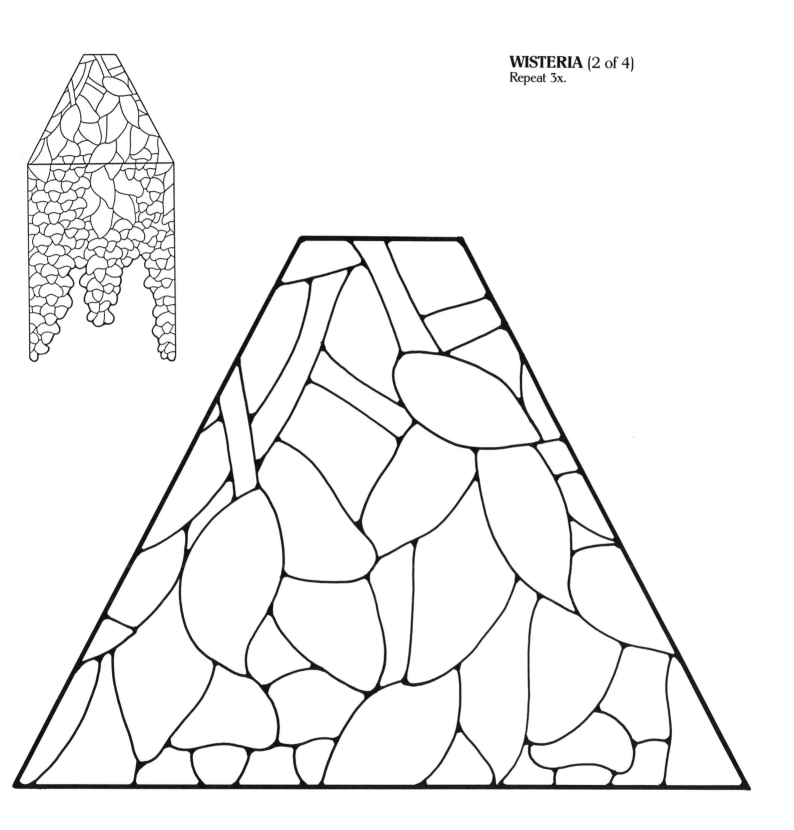

PLATE 23

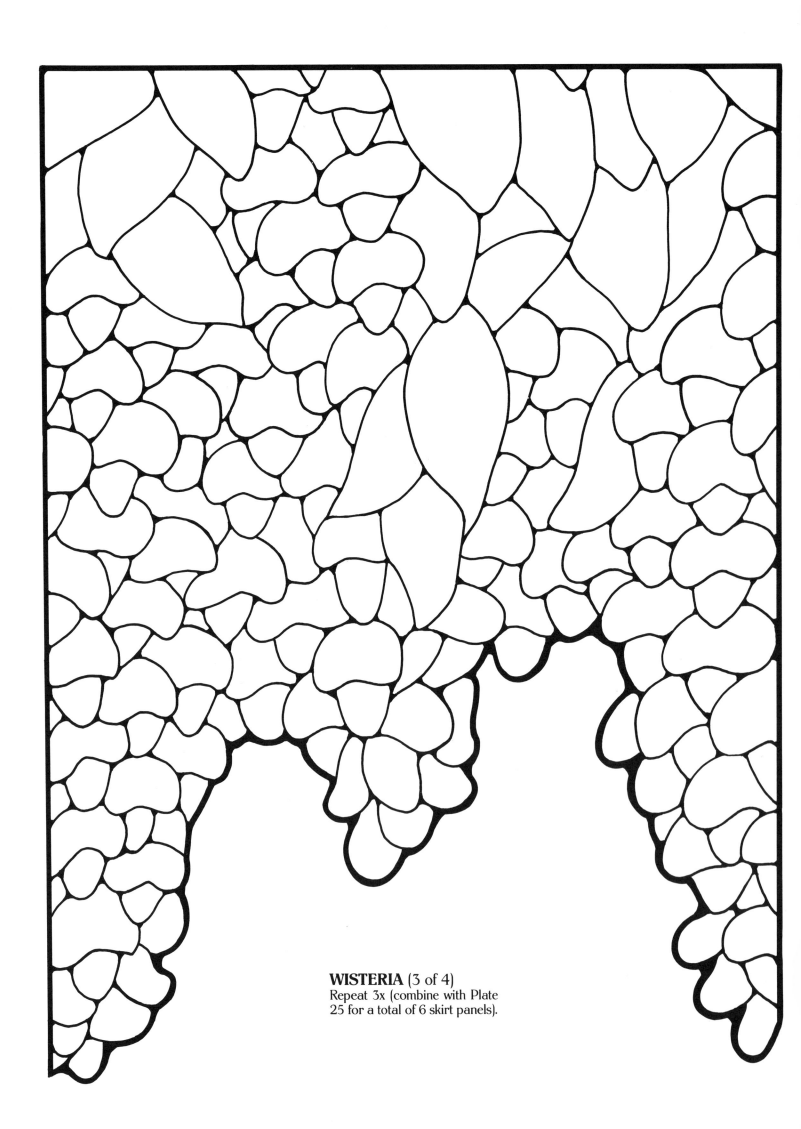

WISTERIA (3 of 4)
Repeat 3x (combine with Plate
25 for a total of 6 skirt panels).

PLATE 24

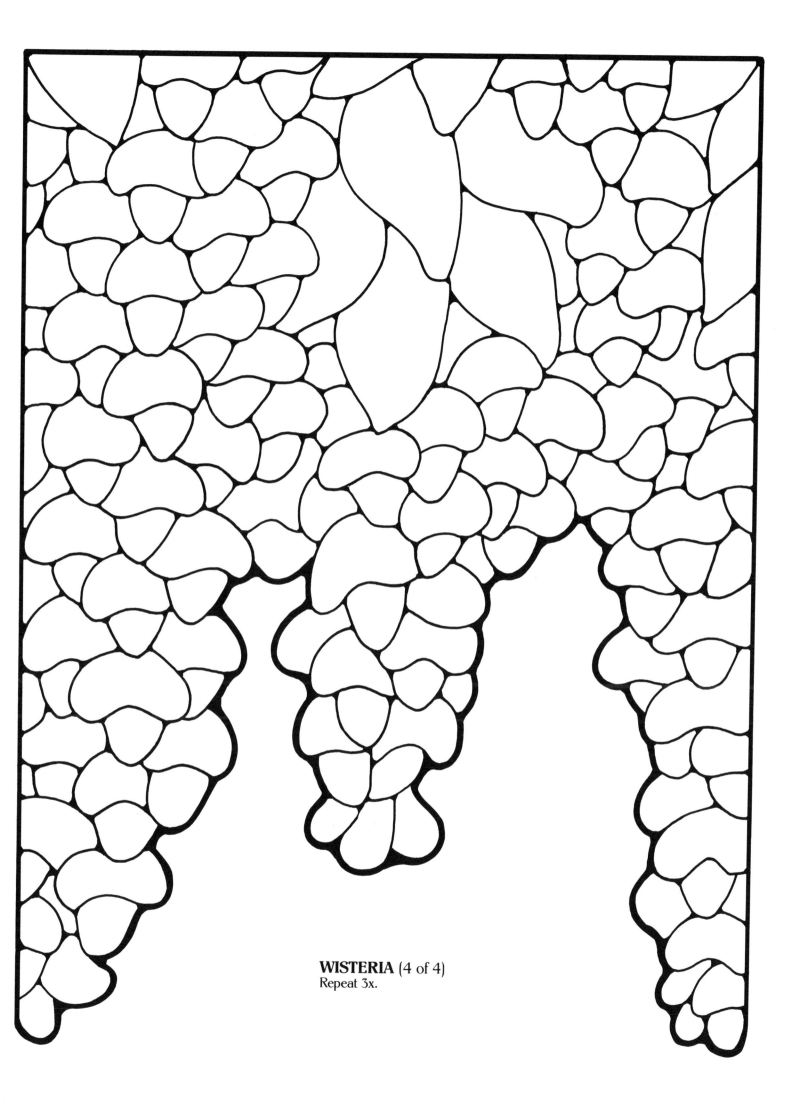

WISTERIA (4 of 4)
Repeat 3x.

PLATE 25

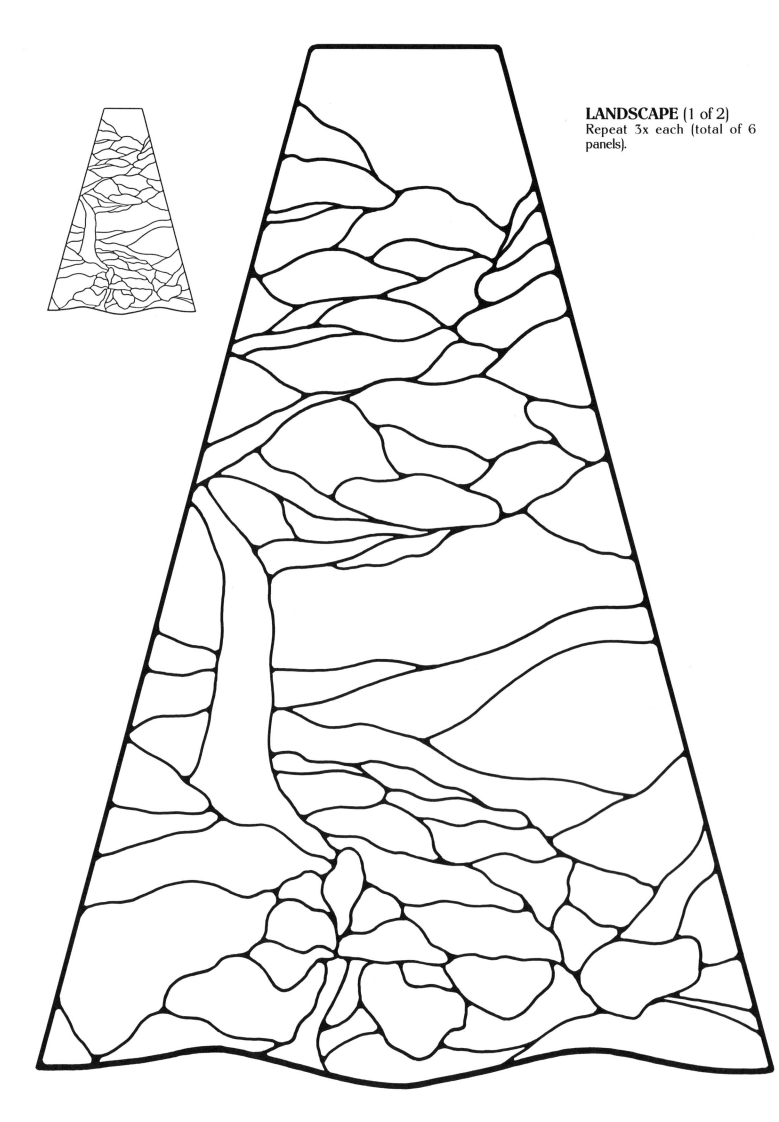

LANDSCAPE (1 of 2)
Repeat 3x each (total of 6 panels).

PLATE 26

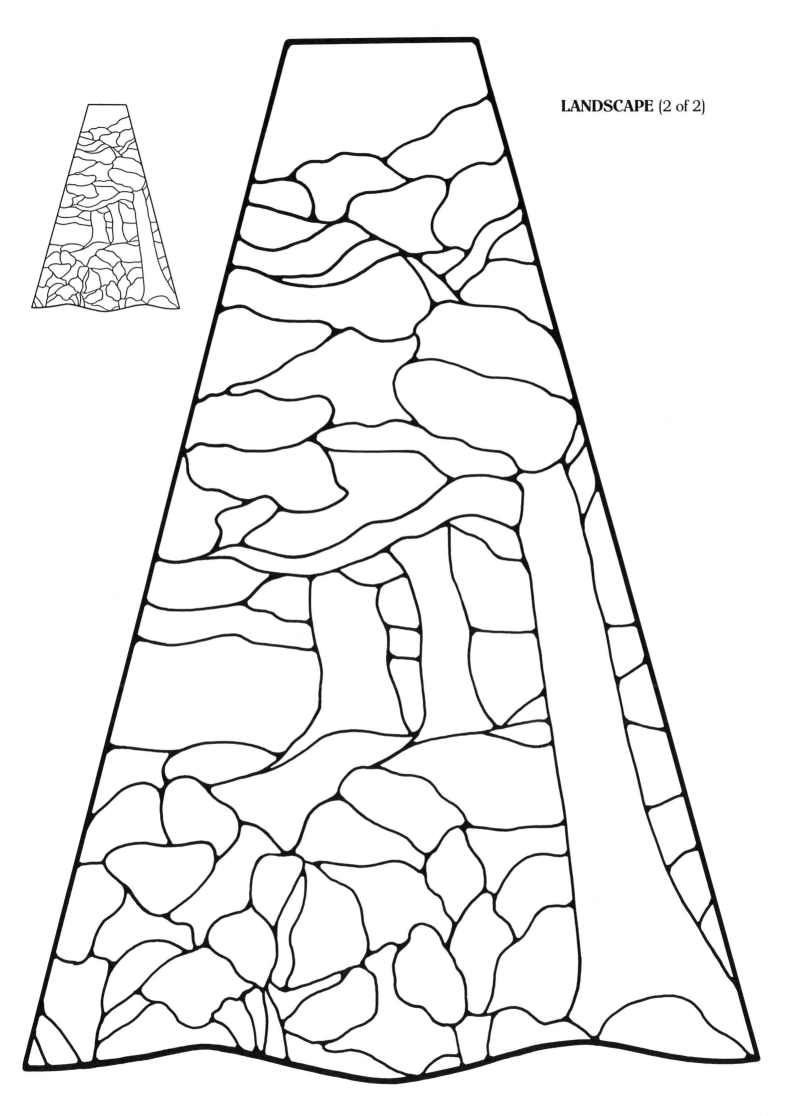

PLATE 27

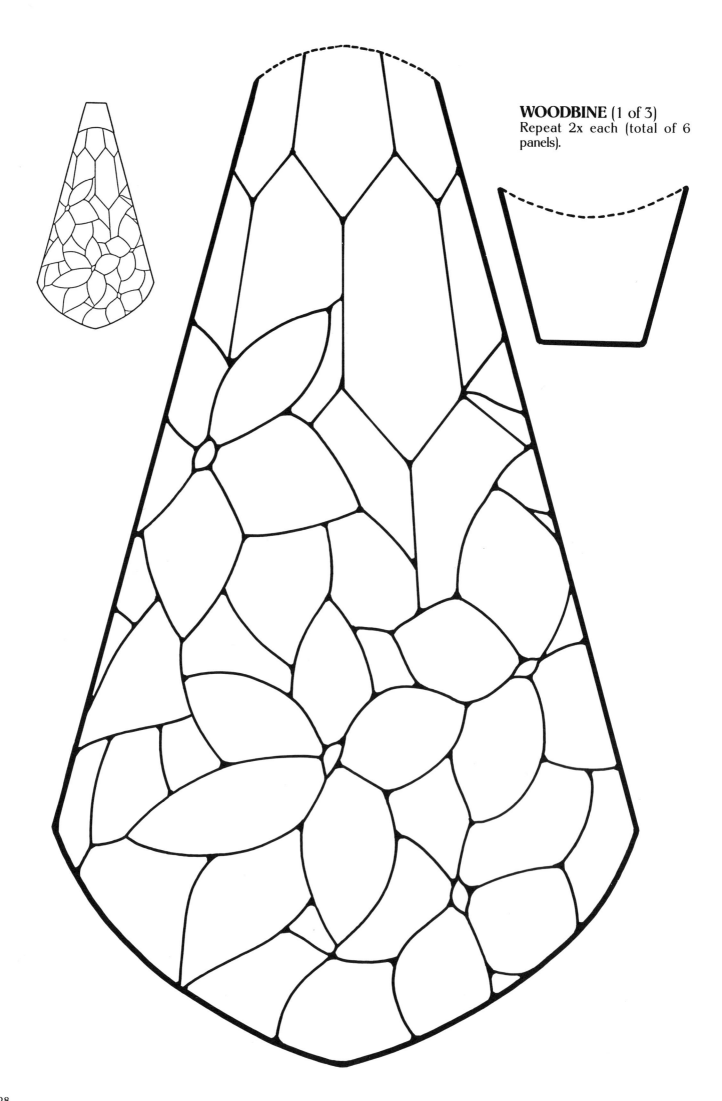

WOODBINE (1 of 3)
Repeat 2x each (total of 6 panels).

PLATE 28

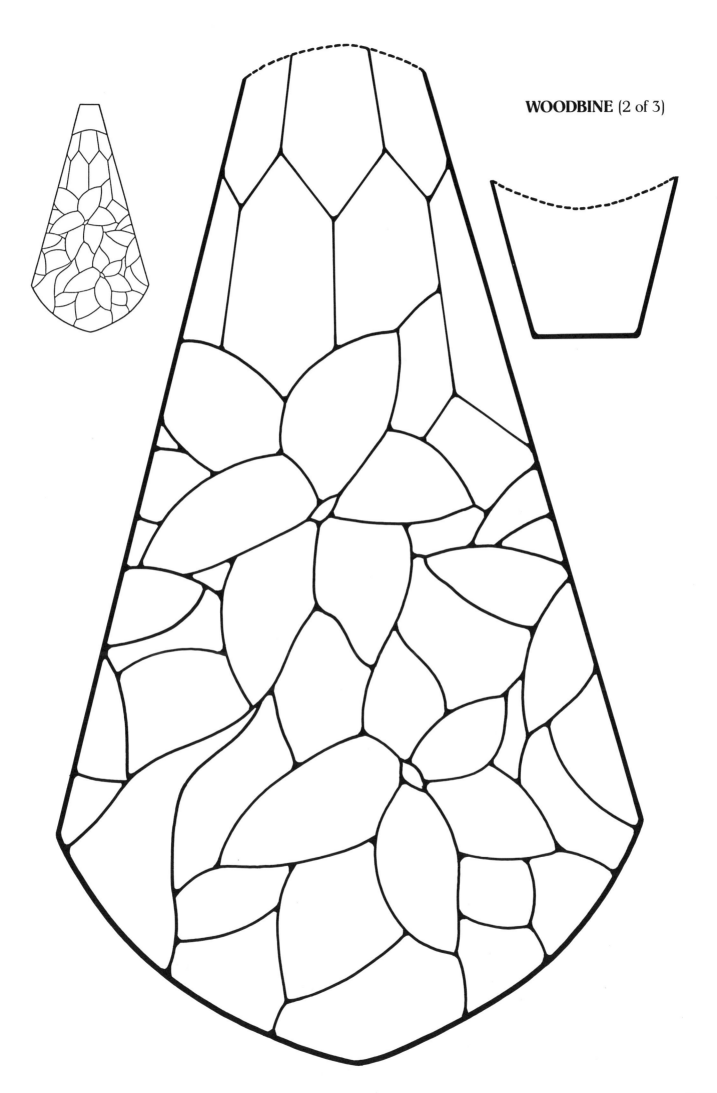

PLATE 29

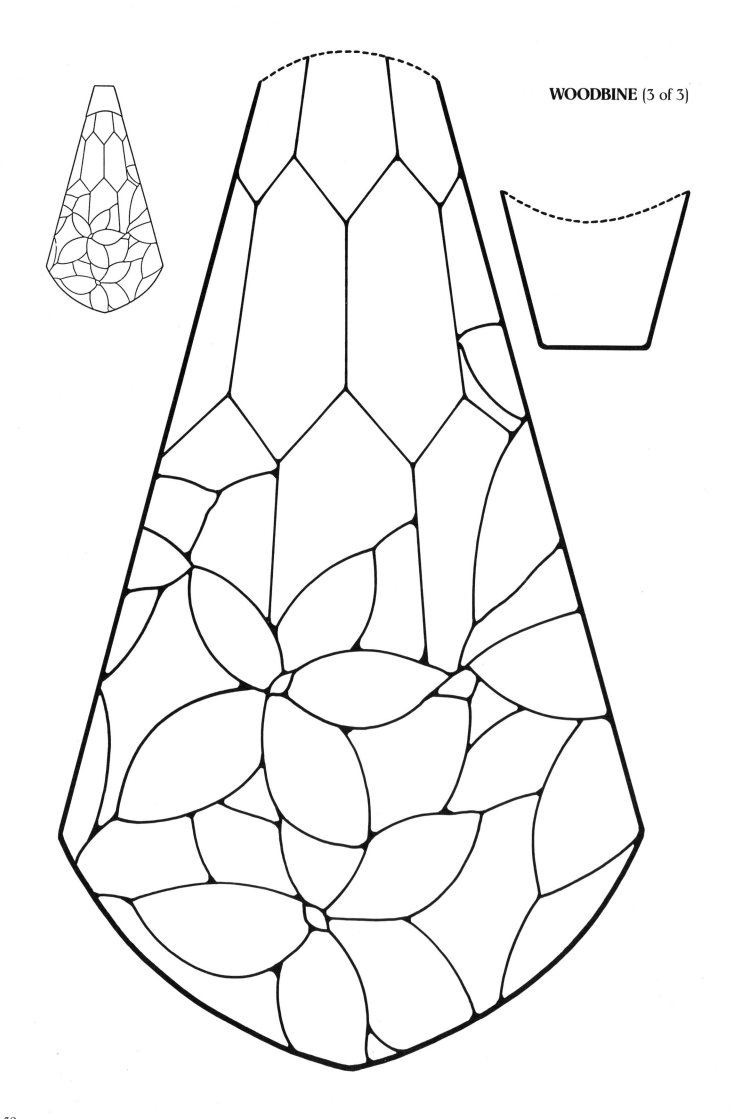

PLATE 30